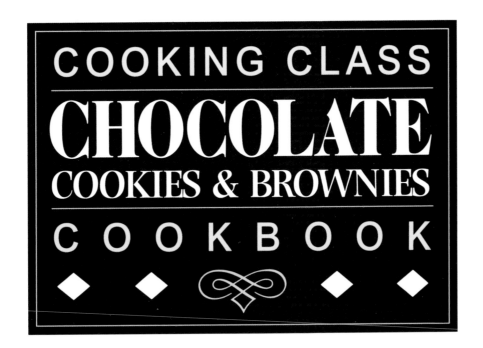

COOKING CLASS
CHOCOLATE
COOKIES & BROWNIES
COOKBOOK

PUBLICATIONS INTERNATIONAL, LTD.

Recipe Development: Karen A. Levin

Photography: Sacco Productions Limited, Chicago.
Pictured on the front cover: Special Treat No-Bake Squares *(page 38).*
Pictured on the inside front cover: Black and White Cut-Outs *(page 50).*
Pictured on the back cover: Double-Dipped Chocolate Peanut Butter Cookies *(page 32).*

ISBN: 0-7853-0667-6

Manufactured in U.S.A.

8 7 6 5 4 3 2 1

CONTENTS

Quick Chocolate Softies (*page 8*)

Fudgy Bittersweet Brownie Pie (*page 62*)

Chocolate Edged Lace Cookies (*page 90*)

CLASS NOTES

Melt-in-your-mouth cookies made with heavenly chocolate is an unbeatable combination. *Cooking Class Chocolate Cookies and Brownies* teaches you the basic techniques to prepare and bake delectable chocolate cookies and brownies. For those who would like to expand their cookie baking skills, we've also included easy-to-follow directions for special touches, such as pinwheel, cut-out, checkerboard and sandwich cookies.

TYPES OF COOKIES

There are five basic types of cookies: bar, drop, refrigerator, rolled and shaped. These types are determined by the consistency of the dough and how it is formed into cookies.

Bar Cookies: Always use the pan size called for in the recipe. Using a different size will affect the cookies' texture; a smaller pan will give a more cakelike texture and a larger pan will give a drier texture.

Drop Cookies: Cookies that are uniform in size and shape will finish baking at the same time. To easily shape drop cookies into a uniform size, use an ice cream scoop with a release bar. The bar usually has a number on it indicating the number of scoops that can be made from one quart of ice cream. The handiest size for cookies is a #80 or #90 scoop. This will yield about one rounded teaspoonful of dough for each cookie.

Refrigerator Cookies: Always shape the dough into rolls before chilling. Shaping is easier if you first place the dough on a piece of waxed paper or plastic wrap. Before chilling, wrap the rolls securely in plastic wrap or air may cause the dough to dry out.

Use gentle pressure and a back-and-forth sawing motion with a sharp knife when slicing the rolls; this helps the cookies keep their nice round shape. Rotating the roll while slicing also keeps one side from flattening.

Rolled Cookies: Chill the cookie dough before rolling for easier handling. Remove only enough dough from the refrigerator to work with at one time. Save any trimmings and reroll them all at once to prevent the dough from becoming tough.

Shaped Cookies: These cookies can be simply hand-shaped into balls or crescents or forced through a cookie press into more complex shapes.

If the recipe calls for a cookie press, do not shape the cookies by hand unless the recipe states that you may do so. The consistency of the dough was created to work in a cookie press.

When using a cookie press, if your first efforts are not succcessful, just place the dough back into the cookie press.

TYPES OF CHOCOLATE

Unsweetened Chocolate: Also called bitter or baking chocolate, this is pure chocolate with no sugar or flavorings added. It is used in baking and is packaged in individually wrapped 1-ounce squares.

Bittersweet Chocolate: This is pure chocolate with some sugar added. Bittersweet chocolate is available in 1-ounce squares or in bars. If unavailable, substitute half unsweetened chocolate and half semisweet chocolate.

Semisweet Chocolate: This is pure chocolate combined with sugar and extra cocoa butter. It is sold in a variety of forms, including 1-ounce squares, bars, chips and chunks.

Milk Chocolate: This is pure chocolate with sugar, extra cocoa butter and milk solids added. It is available in various shapes—bars, chips, stars, etc.

Sweet Cooking Chocolate: This is pure chocolate combined with extra cocoa butter and sugar. It is available in bars.

White Chocolate: This is not considered real chocolate since most or all of the cocoa butter has been removed and replaced by another vegetable fat. White chocolate is available in chips and bars.

Unsweetened Cocoa: This is formed by extracting most of the cocoa butter from pure chocolate and grinding the remaining chocolate solids into a powder. Since most of the cocoa butter is removed, it is low in fat.

GENERAL GUIDELINES

Take the guesswork out of cookie baking by practicing the following techniques:

- Read the entire recipe before you begin.
- Remove butter, margarine and cream cheese from the refrigerator to soften, if necessary.
- Toast and chop nuts, peel and slice fruit and melt chocolate before preparing the dough.

- Measure all the ingredients accurately. Assemble them as stated in the recipe.
- When making bar cookies or brownies, use the pan size specified in the recipe. Prepare the pans according to the recipe directions. Adjust oven racks and preheat the oven. Check oven temperature for accuracy with an oven thermometer.
- Follow recipe directions and baking times. Check doneness with the test given in the recipe.

MEASURING INGREDIENTS

Dry Ingredients: Always use standardized "dry" measuring spoons and "dry" measuring cups. Fill the correct measuring spoon or cup to overflowing and level it off with a metal spatula.

Use "dry" measures to measure flour, brown sugar, granulated sugar, peanut butter, chocolate chips, sour cream, yogurt, nuts, dried fruit, coconut, chopped fresh fruit, preserves and jams.

When measuring flour, lightly spoon it into a measuring cup, then level it off. Do not tap or bang the measuring cup as this will pack the flour.

When measuring brown sugar, pack the sugar by pressing it into the cup. It should be the shape of the cup when turned out.

Liquid Ingredients: Use a standardized glass or plastic measuring cup ("liquid" measuring cup) with a pouring spout. Place the cup on a flat surface, fill to the desired mark. Check measurement at eye level.

When measuring sticky liquids, such as honey and molasses, grease the measuring cup or spray it with vegetable cooking spray before adding the liquid to make removal easier.

BAKING

The best cookie sheets to use have no sides or up to two short sides. They allow the heat to circulate easily during baking and promote even browning.

For even baking and browning place only one cookie sheet at a time in the center of the oven. If the cookies brown unevenly, rotate the cookie sheet from front to back halfway through the baking time.

When baking more than one sheet of cookies at a time, rotate them from top to bottom halfway through the baking time.

For best results, use shortening or a nonstick cooking spray to grease cookie sheets. Or, just line the cookie sheets with parchment paper; it eliminates cleanup, bakes the cookies more evenly and allows them to cool right on the paper instead of on wire racks.

Allow cookie sheets to cool between batches, as the dough spreads if placed on a hot cookie sheet.

To avoid overbaking cookies, check them at the minimum baking time. If more time is needed, watch carefully to make sure they don't burn. It is usually better to slightly underbake than to overbake cookies.

Many cookies should be removed from cookie sheets immediately after baking and placed in a single layer on wire racks to cool. Fragile cookies may need to cool slightly on the cookie sheet before removing to wire racks to cool completely. Bar cookies and brownies may be cooled and stored right in the baking pan.

STORAGE

Unbaked cookie dough can usually be refrigerated for up to one week or frozen for up to six weeks. Label dough with baking information for convenience.

Store soft and crisp cookies separately at room temperature to prevent changes in texture and flavor. Keep soft cookies in airtight containers. If they begin to dry out, add a piece of apple or bread to the container to help them retain moisture. If crisp cookies become soggy, heat undecorated cookies in a 300°F oven for 3 to 5 minutes.

Store cookies with sticky glazes, fragile decorations and icings in single layers between sheets of waxed paper. Bar cookies and brownies may be stored in their own baking pan. Cover with foil or plastic wrap when cool.

As a rule, crisp cookies freeze better than soft, moist cookies. Rich, buttery bar cookies and brownies are an exception to this rule since they freeze extremely well. Baked cookies can be frozen in airtight containers or freezer bags for up to three months. Meringue-based cookies do not freeze well and chocolate-dipped cookies may discolor if frozen. Thaw cookies and brownies unwrapped at room temperature.

Quick Chocolate Softies

1 package (18.25 ounces) devil's
  food chocolate cake mix
1/3 cup water
1/4 cup butter or margarine,
  softened
1 large egg
1 cup large vanilla baking chips
1/2 cup coarsely chopped walnuts

1. Preheat oven to 350°F. Lightly grease cookie sheets.

2. Combine cake mix, water, butter and egg in large bowl. Beat with electric mixer at low speed until moistened, scraping down side of bowl once. Increase speed to medium; beat 1 minute, scraping down side of bowl once. (Dough will be thick.) Stir in chips and walnuts with mixing spoon until well blended.

3. Drop heaping *teaspoonfuls* of dough 2 inches apart (for smaller cookies) or heaping *tablespoonfuls* of dough 3 inches apart (for larger cookies) onto prepared cookie sheets.

4. Bake 10 to 12 minutes or until set. Let cookies stand on cookie sheets 1 minute. Remove cookies with spatula to wire racks; cool completely.

5. Store tightly covered at room temperature or freeze up to 3 months.

*Makes about 2 dozen large
or 4 dozen small cookies*

Prep. time: 15 min.

Step 1. Lightly greasing cookie sheet.

Step 3. Placing heaping teaspoonfuls of dough on cookie sheet.

Step 4. Removing cookies to wire rack.

Chocolate-Pecan Angels

1 cup pecans
1 large egg
1 cup mini semisweet chocolate chips
1 cup sifted powdered sugar (page 72)

1. Preheat oven to 350°F. Lightly grease cookie sheets* or line with parchment paper; set aside.

2. To toast pecans, spread on baking sheet. Bake 8 to 10 minutes or until golden brown, stirring frequently. Remove pecans from pan and cool; set aside. Chop with chef's knife to make 1 cup.

3. To separate egg white from yolk, gently tap egg in center against hard surface, such as side of bowl. Holding a shell half in each hand, gently transfer yolk back and forth between the 2 halves. Allow white to drip down between the 2 halves into bowl. When all white has dripped into bowl, place yolk in another bowl. Store unused egg yolk, covered with water, in airtight container. Refrigerate up to 3 days.

4. Combine chips, pecans and powdered sugar in medium bowl. Add egg white; mix well.

5. Drop teaspoonfuls of batter 2 inches apart onto prepared cookie sheets.

6. Bake 11 to 12 minutes or until edges are light golden brown. Let cookies stand on cookie sheets 1 minute. Remove cookies with spatula to wire racks; cool completely. Or, lift parchment paper from cookie sheets and place directly on countertop.

7. Store tightly covered at room temperature. These cookies do not freeze well.

Makes about 3 dozen cookies

*For best results, use air-cushioned or heavy nonstick cookie sheets.

Prep. time: 20 min.

Step 2. Toasting pecans.

Step 3. Separating an egg.

Step 5. Placing teaspoonfuls of batter 2 inches apart on cookie sheet.

Peanut Butter Chocolate Chippers

1 cup creamy or chunky peanut
  butter
1 cup firmly packed light brown
  sugar
1 large egg
³/₄ cup milk chocolate chips
  Granulated sugar

1. Preheat oven to 350°F.

2. Combine peanut butter, brown sugar and egg in medium bowl with mixing spoon until well blended. Add chips; mix well.

3. Roll heaping tablespoonfuls of dough into 1¹/₂-inch balls. Place balls 2 inches apart on *ungreased* cookie sheets.

4. Dip table fork into granulated sugar; press criss-cross fashion onto each ball, flattening to ¹/₂-inch thickness.

5. Bake 12 minutes or until set. Let cookies stand on cookie sheets 2 minutes. Remove cookies with spatula to wire racks; cool completely.

6. Store tightly covered at room temperature or freeze up to 3 months.

Makes about 2 dozen cookies

Prep. time: 10 min.

Step 3. Rolling dough into ¹/₂-inch balls.

Step 4. Pressing fork into dough to form criss-cross pattern.

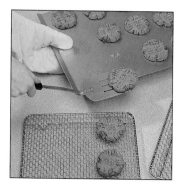

Step 5. Removing cookies to wire racks.

Chocolate Chip Macaroons

2½ cups flaked coconut
⅔ cup mini semisweet chocolate chips
⅔ cup sweetened condensed milk
1 teaspoon vanilla

1. Preheat oven to 350°F. Grease cookie sheets; set aside.

2. Combine coconut, chips, milk and vanilla in medium bowl; stir with mixing spoon until well blended.

3. Drop rounded teaspoonfuls of dough 2 inches apart onto prepared cookie sheets.

4. Press dough gently with back of spoon to flatten slightly.

5. Bake 10 to 12 minutes or until light golden brown. Let cookies stand on cookie sheets 1 minute. Remove cookies with spatula to wire racks; cool completely.

6. Store tightly covered at room temperature. These cookies do not freeze well.

Makes about 3½ dozen cookies

Prep. time: 10 min.

Step 1. Greasing cookie sheet with nonstick cooking spray.

Step 3. Placing rounded teaspoonfuls of dough on cookie sheet.

Step 4. Pressing dough to flatten slightly.

No-Fuss Bar Cookies

24 graham cracker squares
1 cup semisweet chocolate chips
1 cup flaked coconut
$3/4$ cup coarsely chopped walnuts
1 can (14 ounces) sweetened
  condensed milk

1. Preheat oven to 350°F. Grease 13×9-inch baking pan; set aside.

2. Place graham crackers in food processor. Process until crackers form fine crumbs. Measure 2 cups crumbs.

3. Combine crumbs, chips, coconut and walnuts in medium bowl; stir to blend. Add milk; stir with mixing spoon until blended.

4. Spread batter evenly into prepared pan.

5. Bake 15 to 18 minutes or until edges are golden brown. Let pan stand on wire rack until completely cooled. Cut into $2^1/4 × 2^1/4$-inch bars.

6. Store tightly covered at room temperature or freeze up to 3 months.

Makes 20 bars

Prep. time: 10 min.

Step 2. Processing graham crackers in food processor to form fine crumbs.

Step 4. Spreading batter in pan.

Step 5. Cutting into bars.

Ultimate Chippers

2½ cups all-purpose flour
  1 teaspoon baking soda
  ½ teaspoon salt
  1 cup butter or margarine,
    softened
  1 cup packed light brown sugar
  ½ cup granulated sugar
  2 large eggs
  1 tablespoon vanilla
  1 cup semisweet chocolate chips
  1 cup milk chocolate chips
  1 cup vanilla chips
  ½ cup coarsely chopped pecans
    (optional)

1. Preheat oven to 375°F.

2. Place flour, baking soda and salt in medium bowl; stir to combine.

3. Beat butter, brown sugar and granulated sugar in large bowl with electric mixer at medium speed until light and fluffy, scraping down side of bowl once. Beat in eggs and vanilla, scraping down side of bowl once. Add flour mixture. Beat at low speed, scraping down side of bowl once.

4. Stir in chips and pecans with mixing spoon.

5. Drop heaping teaspoonfuls of dough 2 inches apart onto *ungreased* cookie sheets.*

6. Bake 10 to 12 minutes or until edges are golden brown. Let cookies stand on cookie sheets 2 minutes. Remove cookies with spatula to wire racks; cool completely.

7. Store tightly covered at room temperature or freeze up to 3 months.

Makes about 6 dozen cookies

*Or, use a small ice cream scoop (#90) filled with dough and pressed against side of bowl to level.

Step 3. Scraping down side of bowl.

Step 5. Placing dough on cookie sheet with ice cream scoop.

Step 7. Storing cookies.

Oatmeal Candied Chippers

¾ cup all-purpose flour
¾ teaspoon salt
½ teaspoon baking soda
¾ cup butter or margarine,
    softened
¾ cup granulated sugar
¾ cup packed light brown sugar
3 tablespoons milk
1 large egg
2 teaspoons vanilla
3 cups uncooked quick-cooking
    or old-fashioned oats
1⅓ cups (10-ounce package)
    candy-coated semisweet
    chocolate chips*

*Or, substitute 1 cup (8-ounce package)
candy coated milk chocolate chips.

1. Preheat oven to 375°F. Grease cookie sheets; set aside.

2. Place flour, salt and baking soda in small bowl; stir to combine.

3. Beat butter, granulated sugar and brown sugar in large bowl with electric mixer at medium speed until light and fluffy, scraping down side of bowl. Add milk, egg and vanilla; beat well, scraping down side of bowl once. Add flour mixture. Beat at low speed, scraping down side of bowl once.

4. Stir in oats with mixing spoon. Stir in chips.

5. Drop dough by tablespoonfuls 2 inches apart on prepared cookie sheets.**

6. Bake 10 to 11 minutes until edges are golden brown. Let cookies stand 2 minutes on cookie sheets. Remove cookies with spatula to wire racks; cool completely.

7. Store tightly covered at room temperature or freeze up to 3 months.

Makes about 4 dozen cookies

**Or, use a small ice cream scoop (#80) filled with dough and pressed against side of bowl to level.

Step 4. Stirring in oats.

Step 5. Placing dough on cookie sheet with ice cream scoop.

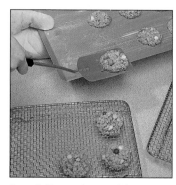
Step 6. Removing cookies to wire rack.

Almond Milk Chocolate Chippers

½ cup slivered almonds
1¼ cups all-purpose flour
½ teaspoon baking soda
½ teaspoon salt
½ cup butter or margarine, softened
½ cup firmly packed light brown sugar
⅓ cup granulated sugar
1 large egg
2 tablespoons almond-flavored liqueur
1 cup milk chocolate chips

1. Preheat oven to 350°F. To toast almonds, spread on baking sheet. Bake 8 to 10 minutes or until golden brown, stirring frequently. Remove almonds from pan and cool; set aside.

2. *Increase oven temperature to 375°F.*

3. Place flour, baking soda and salt in small bowl; stir to combine.

4. Beat butter, brown sugar and granulated sugar in large bowl with electric mixer at medium speed until light and fluffy, scraping down side of bowl once. Beat in egg until well blended. Beat in liqueur. Gradually add flour mixture. Beat at low speed until well blended, scraping down side of bowl once.

5. Stir in chips and almonds with mixing spoon.

6. Drop rounded teaspoonfuls of dough 2 inches apart onto *ungreased* cookie sheets.

7. Bake 9 to 10 minutes or until edges are golden brown. Let cookies stand on cookie sheets 2 minutes. Remove cookies with spatula to wire racks; cool completely.

8. Store tightly covered at room temperature or freeze up to 3 months.

Makes about 3 dozen cookies

Step 4. Scraping down side of bowl.

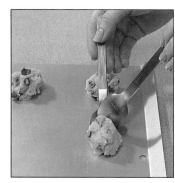

Step 6. Placing rounded teaspoonfuls of dough on cookie sheet.

Step 7. Removing cookies to wire rack.

Chocolate Chip Shortbread

½ cup butter,* softened
½ cup sugar
 1 teaspoon vanilla
 1 cup all-purpose flour
¼ teaspoon salt
½ cup mini semisweet chocolate
   chips

*For best flavor, do not substitute margarine for butter.

1. Preheat oven to 375°F.

2. Beat butter and sugar in large bowl with electric mixer at medium speed until light and fluffy, scraping down side of bowl occasionally. Beat in vanilla. Add flour and salt. Beat at low speed, scraping down side of bowl once. Stir in chips with mixing spoon.

3. Divide dough in half. Press each half into *ungreased* 8-inch round cake pan.

4. Bake 12 minutes or until edges are golden brown. Score shortbread with sharp knife, taking care not to cut completely through shortbread. Make 8 wedges per pan.

5. Let pans stand on wire racks 10 minutes. Invert shortbread onto wire racks; cool completely. Break into wedges.

6. Store tightly covered at room temperature or freeze up to 3 months.

Makes 16 cookies

Step 3. Pressing dough into cake pan.

Step 4. Scoring into wedges.

Step 5. Breaking into wedges.

Banana Chocolate Chip Softies

1 ripe, medium banana
1¼ cups all-purpose flour
1 teaspoon baking powder
½ teaspoon salt
⅓ cup butter or margarine,
    softened
⅓ cup granulated sugar
⅓ cup firmly packed light brown
    sugar
1 large egg
1 teaspoon vanilla
1 cup milk chocolate chips
½ cup coarsely chopped walnuts
    (optional)

1. Preheat oven to 375°F. Lightly grease cookie sheets.

2. Peel banana and place in small bowl. Mash enough banana with fork to measure ½ cup. Set aside.

3. Place flour, baking powder and salt in small bowl; stir to combine.

4. Beat butter, granulated sugar and brown sugar in large bowl with electric mixer at medium speed until light and fluffy, scraping down side of bowl once. Beat in banana, egg and vanilla, scraping down side of bowl once. Add flour mixture. Beat at low speed until well blended, scraping down side of bowl once.

5. Stir in chips and walnuts with mixing spoon. (Dough will be soft.)

6. Drop rounded teaspoonfuls of dough 2 inches apart onto prepared cookie sheets.

7. Bake 9 to 11 minutes or until edges are golden brown. Let cookies stand on cookie sheets 2 minutes. Remove cookies with spatula to wire racks; cool completely.

8. Store tightly covered at room temperature. These cookies do not freeze well.

Makes about 3 dozen cookies

Step 2. Mashing banana with fork.

Step 4. Adding flour mixture to butter mixture.

Step 6. Placing rounded teaspoonfuls of dough on cookie sheet.

Kids' Favorite Jumbo Chippers

2¹/₄ cups all-purpose flour
1 teaspoon baking soda
³/₄ teaspoon salt
1 cup butter or margarine, softened
³/₄ cup granulated sugar
³/₄ cup packed brown sugar
2 large eggs
1 teaspoon vanilla
1 package (12 ounces) mini baking semi-sweet chocolate candies
1 cup peanut butter flavored chips

1. Preheat oven to 375°F.

2. Place flour, baking soda and salt in medium bowl; stir to combine.

3. Beat butter, granulated sugar and brown sugar in large bowl with electric mixer at medium speed until light and fluffy, scraping down side of bowl once. Beat in eggs and vanilla, scraping down side of bowl once. Add flour mixture. Beat at low speed until well blended, scraping down side of bowl once.

4. Stir in candies and chips with mixing spoon.

5. Drop heaping tablespoonfuls of dough 3 inches apart onto *ungreased* cookie sheets.

6. Bake 10 to 12 minutes or until edges are golden brown. Let cookies stand on cookie sheets 2 minutes. Remove cookies with spatula to wire racks; cool completely.

7. Store tightly covered at room temperature or freeze up to 3 months.

Makes 3 dozen jumbo cookies

Step 3. Scraping down side of bowl.

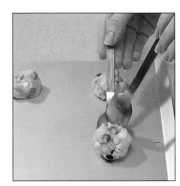

Step 5. Placing heaping tablespoonfuls of dough on cookie sheet.

Step 6. Removing cookies to wire rack.

Orange-Walnut Chippers

½ cup all-purpose flour
¼ teaspoon baking soda
¼ teaspoon salt
½ cup butter or margarine,
  softened
1 cup packed light brown sugar
1 large egg
1 tablespoon orange peel
1½ cups uncooked quick-cooking
  or old-fashioned oats
1 cup semisweet chocolate chips
½ cup coarsely chopped walnuts

1. Preheat oven to 375°F. Lightly grease cookie sheets; set aside.

2. Place flour, baking soda and salt in small bowl; stir to combine.

3. Beat butter and sugar in large bowl with electric mixer at medium speed until light and fluffy, scraping down side of bowl once. Beat in egg and orange peel, scraping down side of bowl once. Add flour mixture. Beat at low speed, scraping down side of bowl once.

4. Stir in oats with mixing spoon. Stir in chips and nuts.

5. Drop teaspoonfuls of dough 2 inches apart onto prepared cookie sheets.

6. Bake 10 to 12 minutes or until golden brown. Let cookies stand on cookie sheets 2 minutes. Remove cookies with spatula to wire racks; cool completely.

7. Store tightly covered at room temperature or freeze up to 3 months.

Makes about 3 dozen cookies

Step 1. Lightly greasing cookie sheet.

Step 5. Placing teaspoonfuls of dough on cookie sheet.

Step 6. Removing cookies to wire rack.

Double-Dipped Chocolate Peanut Butter Cookies

1¼ cups all-purpose flour
½ teaspoon baking powder
½ teaspoon baking soda
½ teaspoon salt
½ cup butter or margarine, softened
  Granulated sugar
½ cup packed light brown sugar
½ cup creamy or chunky peanut butter
1 large egg
1 teaspoon vanilla
1½ cups semisweet chocolate chips
1½ cups milk chocolate chips
3 teaspoons shortening, divided

1. Preheat oven to 350°F. Place flour, baking powder, baking soda and salt in bowl; stir.

2. Beat butter, ½ cup granulated sugar and brown sugar in large bowl with electric mixer at medium speed until light and fluffy, scraping down side of bowl once. Beat in peanut butter, egg and vanilla, scraping down side of bowl once. Gradually stir in flour mixture with mixing spoon, blending well.

3. Roll heaping tablespoonfuls of dough into 1½-inch balls. Place balls 2 inches apart on *ungreased* cookie sheets. (If dough is too soft to roll into balls, refrigerate 30 minutes.)

4. Dip table fork into granulated sugar; press criss-cross fashion onto each ball, flattening to ½-inch thickness.

5. Bake 12 minutes or until set. Let cookies stand on cookie sheets 2 minutes. Remove cookies with spatula to wire rack; cool.

6. Melt semisweet chocolate chips and 1½ teaspoons shortening in top of double boiler over hot, not boiling, water. Dip one end of each cookie one third the way up; place on waxed paper. Let stand until chocolate is set, about 30 minutes.

7. Melt milk chocolate chips with 1½ teaspoons shortening in top of double boiler over hot, not boiling, water. Dip opposite end of each cookie one third the way up; place on waxed paper. Let stand until chocolate is set, about 30 minutes.

8. Store cookies between sheets of waxed paper at cool room temperature or freeze up to 3 months.

Makes about 2 dozen 3-inch cookies

Step 4. Pressing fork into dough to form a criss-cross pattern.

Step 7. Dipping cookie one third the way into melted chocolate.

Surprise Cookies

**2 squares (1 ounce each)
semisweet chocolate, coarsely
chopped**
1¼ cups all-purpose flour
½ teaspoon baking powder
¼ teaspoon salt
**½ cup butter or margarine,
softened**
½ cup sugar
1 large egg
1 teaspoon vanilla
**Fillings as desired: maraschino
cherries (well drained) or
candied cherries; chocolate
mint candies, broken in half;
white baking bar, cut into
chunks; thick milk chocolate
candy bar, cut into chunks, or
semi-sweet chocolate chunks;
raspberry jam or apricot
preserves**
Nonpareils, for garnish

1. Preheat oven to 350°F. Grease mini-muffin cups; set aside.

2. Melt chocolate in small, heavy saucepan over low heat, stirring constantly; set aside.

3. Place flour, baking powder and salt in small bowl; stir to combine.

4. Beat butter and sugar in large bowl with electric mixer at medium speed until light and fluffy, scraping down side of bowl once. Beat in egg and vanilla, scraping down side of bowl once. Gradually beat in chocolate. Gradually add flour mixture. Beat at low speed, scraping down side of bowl once.

5. Drop level teaspoonfuls of dough into prepared muffin cups. Smooth down dough and form small indentation with back of teaspoon.

6. Fill as desired with assorted filling ingredients. Top with heaping teaspoonful of dough, smoothing top lightly with back of spoon. Sprinkle tops with nonpareils, if desired.

7. Bake 15 to 17 minutes or until centers of cookies are set. Remove pan to wire rack; cool completely before removing cookies from pan.

8. Store tightly covered at room temperature. These cookies do not freeze well.

Makes 1 dozen cookies

Step 2. Melting chocolate in saucepan.

Step 5. Forming small indentation in dough with back of spoon.

Step 6. Smoothing top of dough.

Marshmallow Sandwich Cookies

2 cups all-purpose flour
¹/₂ cup unsweetened cocoa powder
2 teaspoons baking soda
¹/₄ teaspoon salt
²/₃ cup butter or margarine,
    softened
    Sugar
¹/₄ cup light corn syrup
1 large egg
1 teaspoon vanilla
24 large marshmallows

1. Preheat oven to 350°F.

2. Place flour, cocoa, baking soda and salt in medium bowl; stir to combine.

3. Beat butter and 1¹/₄ cups sugar in large bowl with electric mixer at medium speed until light and fluffy, scraping down side of bowl once. Beat in corn syrup, egg and vanilla, scraping down side of bowl once. Gradually add flour mixture. Beat at low speed, scraping down side of bowl occasionally. Cover and refrigerate dough 15 minutes or until firm enough to roll into balls.

4. Place sugar in shallow dish. Roll tablespoonfuls of dough into 1-inch balls; roll in sugar to coat. Place 3 inches apart on *ungreased* cookie sheets.

5. Bake 10 to 11 minutes or until set. Remove cookies with spatula to wire rack; cool completely.

6. To assemble sandwiches,* place 1 marshmallow on flat side of 1 cookie on paper plate. Microwave at HIGH 12 seconds or until marshmallow is hot.

7. Immediately place another cookie, flat side down, over marshmallow; press together slightly.

8. Store tightly covered at room temperature. These cookies do not freeze well.
Makes 2 dozen sandwich cookies

*Cookies also taste great just as they are!

Step 4. Rolling dough balls in sugar to coat.

Step 6. Placing marshmallow on cookie.

Step 7. Forming sandwich.

Special Treat No-Bake Squares

Crust
- **½ cup butter or margarine**
- **¼ cup granulated sugar**
- **¼ cup unsweetened cocoa powder**
- **1 large egg**
- **¼ teaspoon salt**
- **1½ cups graham cracker crumbs (about 18 graham crackers)**
- **¾ cup flaked coconut**
- **½ cup chopped pecans**

Filling
- **⅓ cup butter or margarine, softened**
- **1 package (3 ounces) cream cheese, softened**
- **1 teaspoon vanilla**
- **1 cup powdered sugar**

Glaze
- **2 ounces dark sweet or bittersweet chocolate candy bar, broken into ½-inch pieces**
- **1 teaspoon butter or margarine**

1. Line 9-inch square pan with foil, shiny side up, allowing 2-inch overhang on sides. (The overhang allows cookie to be lifted out of pan for easier cutting.) Or, lightly grease pan. Set aside.

2. For crust, combine ½ cup butter, granulated sugar, cocoa, egg and salt in medium saucepan. Cook over medium heat, stirring constantly, until mixture thickens, about 2 minutes.

3. Remove from heat; stir in graham cracker crumbs, coconut and pecans. Press evenly into prepared pan.

4. For filling, beat ⅓ cup butter, cream cheese and vanilla in small bowl with electric mixer at medium speed until smooth, scraping down side of bowl once. Gradually beat in powdered sugar. Spread over crust; refrigerate 30 minutes.

5. For glaze, combine candy bar and 1 teaspoon butter in small resealable plastic freezer bag; seal bag. Microwave at HIGH 50 seconds. Turn bag over; microwave at HIGH 40 to 50 seconds or until melted. Knead bag until candy bar is smooth. (Technique on page 52.)

6. Cut off very tiny corner of bag; drizzle chocolate over filling. Refrigerate until firm, about 20 minutes.

7. Remove bars from pan, using foil. Cut into 1½-inch squares. Store tightly covered in refrigerator.

Makes 25 squares

Step 4. Spreading filling over crust.

Step 6. Drizzling chocolate over filling.

Choco Cheesecake Squares

1/3 cup butter or margarine, softened

1/3 cup packed light brown sugar

1 cup *plus* 1 tablespoon all-purpose flour, divided

1/2 cup chopped pecans (optional)

1 cup semisweet chocolate chips

1 package (8 ounces) cream cheese, softened

1/4 cup granulated sugar

1 large egg

1 teaspoon vanilla

1 tablespoon powdered sugar

1 tablespoon unsweetened cocoa powder

1. Preheat oven to 350°F. Grease 8-inch square baking pan; set aside.

2. Beat butter and brown sugar in large bowl with electric mixer at medium speed until light and fluffy, scraping down side of bowl once. Add 1 cup flour. Beat at low speed, scraping down side of bowl once. Stir in pecans with mixing spoon. (Mixture will be crumbly.) Press evenly into prepared pan.

3. Bake 15 minutes.

4. Place chips in 1-cup glass measure. Microwave at HIGH 2½ to 3 minutes or until melted, stirring after 2 minutes.

5. Beat cream cheese and granulated sugar in medium bowl with electric mixer at medium speed until light and fluffy, scraping down side of bowl once. Add remaining 1 tablespoon flour, egg and vanilla; beat at low speed until smooth. Gradually stir in melted chocolate, mixing well.

6. Pour cream cheese mixture over partially baked crust. Return to oven; bake 15 minutes or until set.

7. Remove pan to wire rack; cool completely. Combine powdered sugar and cocoa in cup. Place in fine-mesh strainer; sprinkle over brownies, if desired. Cut brownies into 2-inch squares.

8. Store tightly covered in refrigerator or freeze up to 3 months.

Makes 16 squares

Step 2. Scraping down side of bowl.

Step 4. Stirring melted chocolate chips.

Step 6. Pouring cream cheese mixture over crust.

Chocolate Caramel Pecan Bars

2 cups butter, softened, divided
½ cup granulated sugar
1 large egg
2¾ cups all-purpose flour
⅔ cup packed light brown sugar
¼ cup light corn syrup
2½ cups coarsely chopped pecans
1 cup semisweet chocolate chips

1. Preheat oven to 375°F. Grease 15 × 10-inch jelly-roll pan; set aside.

2. Beat 1 cup butter and granulated sugar in large bowl with electric mixer at medium speed until light and fluffy, scraping down side of bowl once. Beat in egg. Add flour. Beat at low speed, scraping down side of bowl once. Pat dough into prepared pan.

3. Bake 20 minutes or until light golden brown.

4. While bars are baking, prepare topping. Combine remaining 1 cup butter, brown sugar and corn syrup in medium, heavy saucepan. Cook over medium heat until mixture boils, stirring frequently. Boil gently 2 minutes, without stirring. Quickly stir in pecans and spread topping evenly over base. Return to oven and bake 20 minutes or until dark golden brown and bubbling.

5. Immediately sprinkle chocolate chips evenly over hot caramel. Gently press chips into caramel topping with spatula. Loosen caramel from edges of pan with a thin spatula or knife.

6. Remove pan to wire rack; cool completely. Cut into 3 × 1½-inch bars.

7. Store tightly covered at room temperature or freeze up to 3 months.

Makes 40 bars

Step 2. Patting dough into pan.

Step 4. Stirring pecans into hot topping.

Step 5. Pressing chips into caramel topping.

Chocolate Macaroons

2 large eggs
12 ounces semisweet baking
  chocolate or chips
1 can (8 ounces) almond paste
1/2 cup powdered sugar
2 tablespoons all-purpose flour
  Powdered sugar for garnish

1. Preheat oven to 300°F. Line cookie sheets with parchment paper; set aside.

2. To separate egg whites from yolks, gently tap egg in center against hard surface, such as side of bowl. Holding a shell half in each hand, gently transfer yolk back and forth between the 2 halves. Allow white to drip down between the 2 halves into bowl. When all white has dripped into bowl, place yolk in another bowl. Transfer white to third bowl. Repeat with remaining egg. Store unused egg yolks, covered with water, in airtight container. Refrigerate up to 3 days.

3. Melt chocolate in small, heavy saucepan over low heat, stirring constantly; set aside.

4. Beat almond paste, egg whites and sugar in large bowl with electric mixer at medium speed 1 minute, scraping down side of bowl once. Beat in chocolate until well combined. Beat in flour at low speed, scraping down side of bowl once.

5. Spoon dough into pastry tube fitted with rosette tip. Pipe 1½-inch spirals 1 inch apart onto prepared cookie sheets. Pipe all cookies at once; dough will get stiff upon standing.

6. Bake 20 minutes or until set. Carefully remove parchment paper to countertop; cool completely.

7. Peel cookies off parchment paper. Place powdered sugar in fine-mesh strainer; sprinkle over cookies, if desired.

8. Store tightly covered at room temperature or freeze up to 3 months.

Makes about 3 dozen cookies

Step 2. Separating an egg.

Step 5. Piping dough onto cookie sheet.

Step 7. Removing cookies from parchment paper.

Chocolate Sugar Spritz

2 squares (1 ounce each)
    unsweetened chocolate,
    coarsely chopped
2¼ cups all-purpose flour
¼ teaspoon salt
1 cup butter or margarine,
    softened
¾ cup granulated sugar
1 large egg
1 teaspoon almond extract
½ cup powdered sugar
1 teaspoon ground cinnamon

1. Preheat oven to 400°F.

2. Melt chocolate in small, heavy saucepan over low heat, stirring constantly; set aside.

3. Combine flour and salt in small bowl; stir to combine.

4. Beat butter and granulated sugar in large bowl with electric mixer at medium speed until light and fluffy, scraping down side of bowl once. Beat in egg and almond extract, scraping down side of bowl. Beat in chocolate. Gradually add flour mixture with mixing spoon. (Dough will be stiff.)

5. Fit cookie press with desired plate (or change plates for different shapes after first batch). Fill press with dough; press dough 1 inch apart onto *ungreased* cookie sheets.

6. Bake 7 minutes or until just set.

7. Combine powdered sugar and cinnamon in small bowl. Transfer to fine-mesh strainer and sprinkle over hot cookies while they are still on cookie sheets. Remove cookies with spatula to wire racks; cool completely.

8. Store tightly covered at room temperature. These cookies do not freeze well.

Makes 4 to 5 dozen cookies

Step 4. Stirring flour into batter.

Step 5. Pressing dough onto cookie sheet.

Step 7. Sprinkling cinnamon-sugar mixture over cookies.

Two-Toned Spritz Cookies

1 square (1 ounce) unsweetened
   chocolate, coarsely chopped
2¼ cups all-purpose flour
¼ teaspoon salt
1 cup butter or margarine,
   softened
1 cup sugar
1 large egg
1 teaspoon vanilla

1. Melt chocolate in small, heavy saucepan over low heat, stirring constantly; set aside.

2. Place flour and salt in medium bowl; stir.

3. Beat butter and sugar in large bowl with electric mixer at medium speed until light and fluffy, scraping down side of bowl once. Beat in egg and vanilla, scraping down side of bowl once. Gradually add flour mixture. Beat at low speed, scraping down side of bowl once.

4. Remove and reserve 2 cups dough. Beat chocolate into dough in bowl until smooth. Flatten each piece of dough into a disc; wrap in plastic wrap and refrigerate 20 minutes or until doughs are easy to handle.

5. Preheat oven to 400°F.

6. Unwrap vanilla dough. Roll out between 2 sheets of waxed paper to ½-inch thickness. Cut into 5 × 4-inch rectangles.

7. Unwrap chocolate dough. Place on sheet of waxed paper. Using waxed paper to hold dough, roll it back and forth to form a log about 1-inch in diameter. Cut into 5-inch-long logs.

8. Place chocolate log in center of vanilla rectangle. Wrap vanilla dough around log and fit into cookie press fitted with star disc.

9. Press dough 1½ inches apart on cold, *ungreased* cookie sheets. (Technique on page 46.)

10. Bake 10 minutes or until just set. Remove cookies with spatula to wire racks; cool.

11. Store tightly covered at room temperature or freeze up to 3 months.

Makes about 4 dozen cookies

Step 6. Rolling out vanilla dough.

Step 7. Rolling chocolate dough into log.

Step 8. Shaping vanilla dough around chocolate log.

Black and White Cut-Outs

2³/₄ cups *plus* 2 tablespoons
    all-purpose flour, divided
1 teaspoon baking soda
³/₄ teaspoon salt
1 cup butter or margarine,
    softened
³/₄ cup granulated sugar
³/₄ cup packed light brown sugar
2 large eggs
1 teaspoon vanilla
¹/₄ cup unsweetened cocoa powder
4 ounces white chocolate baking
    bar, broken into ¹/₂-inch pieces
    Assorted decorative candies
    (optional)
4 ounces semisweet chocolate
    chips

1. Place 2³/₄ cups flour, baking soda and salt in small bowl; stir to combine.

2. Beat butter, granulated sugar and brown sugar in large bowl with electric mixer at medium speed until light and fluffy, scraping down side of bowl once. Beat in eggs, 1 at a time, scraping down side of bowl after each addition. Beat in vanilla. Gradually add flour mixture. Beat at low speed, scraping down side of bowl once.

3. Remove half of dough from bowl; reserve. To make chocolate dough, beat cocoa into remaining dough with mixing spoon until well blended. To make vanilla cookie dough, beat remaining 2 tablespoons flour into reserved dough.

4. Flatten each piece of dough into a disc; wrap in plastic wrap and refrigerate about 1¹/₂ hours or until firm. (Dough may be refrigerated up to 3 days before baking.)

5. Preheat oven to 375°F.

6. Working with 1 type of dough at a time, unwrap dough and place on lightly floured surface. Roll out dough to ¹/₄-inch thickness with floured rolling pin.

continued on page 52

Step 3. Mixing chocolate dough.

Step 4. Wrapping flattened dough in plastic wrap.

Step 6. Rolling out chocolate dough.

Black and White Cut-Outs, continued

7. Cut dough into desired shapes with cookie cutters. Place cut-outs 1 inch apart on *ungreased* cookie sheets.

8. Bake 9 to 11 minutes or until set. Let cookies stand on cookie sheets 2 minutes. Remove cookies with spatula to wire rack; cool completely.

9. For white chocolate drizzle, place baking bar pieces in small resealable plastic freezer bag; seal bag. Microwave at MEDIUM (50% power) 2 minutes. Turn bag over; microwave at MEDIUM (50% power) 2 to 3 minutes or until melted. Knead bag until baking bar is smooth.

10. Cut off very tiny corner of bag; pipe or drizzle baking bar onto chocolate cookies. Decorate as desired with assorted candies. Let stand until white chocolate is set, about 30 minutes.

11. For chocolate drizzle, place chocolate chips in small resealable plastic freezer bag; seal bag. Microwave at HIGH 1 minute. Turn bag over; microwave at HIGH 1 to 2 minutes or until melted. Knead bag until chocolate is smooth.

12. Cut off tiny corner of bag; pipe or drizzle chocolate onto vanilla cookies. Decorate as desired with assorted candies. Let stand until chocolate is set, about 40 minutes.

13. Store tightly covered at room temperature or freeze up to 3 months.
Makes 3 to 4 dozen cookies

Black and White Sandwiches: Cut out both doughs with same cookie cutter. Spread thin layer of prepared frosting on flat side of chocolate cookie. Place flat side of vanilla cookie over frosting. Drizzle either side of cookie with melted chocolate or white chocolate.

Step 7. Cutting out dough.

Step 9. Kneading white chocolate in plastic bag.

Black and White Sandwiches: Making sandwich cookies.

Old-Fashioned Ice Cream Sandwiches

2 squares (1 ounce each)
   semisweet baking chocolate,
   coarsely chopped
1½ cups all-purpose flour
 ¼ teaspoon baking soda
 ¼ teaspoon salt
 ½ cup butter or margarine,
   softened
 ½ cup sugar
 1 large egg
 1 teaspoon vanilla
   Vanilla or mint chocolate chip
   ice cream, softened*

*One quart of ice cream can be softened
in the microwave at HIGH for about 20
seconds.

1. Place chocolate in 1-cup glass measure. Microwave at HIGH 3 to 4 minutes or until chocolate is melted, stirring after 2 minutes; set aside.

2. Place flour, baking soda and salt in small bowl; stir to combine.

3. Beat butter and sugar in large bowl with electric mixer at medium speed until light and fluffy, scraping down side of bowl once.

4. Beat in egg and vanilla, scraping down side of bowl once. Gradually beat in chocolate. Stir in flour mixture with mixing spoon.

5. Form dough into 2 discs; wrap in plastic wrap and refrigerate until firm, at least 2 hours. (Dough may be stored in the refrigerator up to 3 days before baking.)

6. Preheat oven to 350°F. Grease cookie sheet; set aside.

7. Unwrap 1 piece of dough. Roll out to ¼- to ⅛-inch thickness between 2 sheets of waxed paper.

continued on page 54

Step 1. Stirring melted chocolate.

Step 5. Wrapping flattened dough in plastic wrap.

Step 6. Rolling out dough between 2 sheets of waxed paper.

Old-Fashioned Ice Cream Sandwiches, continued

8. Remove top sheet of waxed paper; invert dough onto prepared cookie sheet.

9. Cut through dough down to cookie sheets with paring knife, forming 3 × 2-inch rectangles. Remove excess scraps of dough from edges. Add to second disc of dough and repeat rolling and scoring until dough is used up. Prick each rectangle with table fork, if desired.

10. Bake 10 minutes or until set. Let cookies stand on cookie sheet 1 minute. Cut through score marks with paring knife while cookies are still warm. Remove cookies with spatula to wire racks; cool completely.

11. Spread softened ice cream on flat side of half the cookies; top with remaining cookies.

12. Serve immediately or wrap separately in plastic wrap and freeze up to 1 month.

Makes about 8 ice cream sandwiches

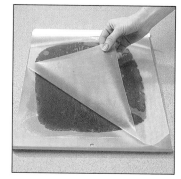

Step 8. Removing top sheet of waxed paper.

Step 9. Cutting dough into rectangles.

Step 11. Spreading ice cream on cookies.

Mint Chocolate Pinwheels

1¼ cups all-purpose flour
1 teaspoon baking powder
½ teaspoon salt
⅔ cup butter or margarine, softened
1 cup sugar
1 large egg
1 teaspoon vanilla
1 cup uncooked quick-cooking oats
1 cup mint chocolate chips

1. Place flour, baking powder and salt in small bowl; stir to combine.

2. Beat butter and sugar in large bowl with electric mixer at medium speed until light and fluffy, scraping down side of bowl once. Add egg and vanilla; beat well, scraping down side of bowl once. Gradually add flour mixture. Beat at low speed, scraping down side of bowl once. Stir in oats with mixing spoon.

3. Place chips in 1-cup glass measure. Microwave at HIGH about 2 minutes or until melted, stirring after 1½ minutes.

4. Divide cookie dough into halves. Add melted chocolate to one half; mix well.

5. Roll out each half of dough between 2 sheets of waxed paper into 15 × 10-inch rectangles. Remove waxed paper from top of each rectangle.

6. Place chocolate dough over plain dough; remove bottom sheet of waxed paper from bottom of chocolate dough. Using bottom sheet of waxed paper as a guide and starting at long side, tightly roll up dough jelly-roll style, removing waxed paper as you roll. Wrap dough in plastic wrap; refrigerate at least 2 hours or up to 24 hours.

7. Preheat oven to 350°F. Lightly grease cookie sheet. Unwrap log. With long, sharp knife, cut dough into ¼-inch slices. Place 3 inches apart on prepared cookie sheet.

8. Bake 10 to 12 minutes or until set. Remove cookies with spatula to wire racks; cool.

9. Store tightly covered at room temperature or freeze up to 3 months.

Makes about 3 dozen cookies

Step 6. Rolling up dough jelly-roll style.

Step 7. Cutting dough into ¼-inch slices.

Chocolate Dipped Cinnamon Thins

1¼ cups all-purpose flour
1½ teaspoons ground cinnamon
¼ teaspoon salt
1 cup unsalted butter, softened
1 cup powdered sugar
1 large egg
1 teaspoon vanilla
4 ounces broken bittersweet
   chocolate candy bar

1. Place flour, cinnamon and salt in bowl; stir.

2. Beat butter in large bowl with electric mixer at medium speed until light and fluffy, scraping down side of bowl once. Add sugar; beat well. Add egg and vanilla; beat well, scraping down side of bowl once. Gradually add flour mixture. Beat at low speed, scraping down side of bowl occasionally.

3. Place dough on sheet of waxed paper. Using waxed paper to hold dough, roll it back and forth to form a log about 12 inches long and 2½ inches wide.

4. Securely wrap log in waxed paper. Refrigerate at least 2 hours or until firm. (Log may be frozen up to 3 months; thaw in refrigerator before baking.)

5. Preheat oven to 350°F. Cut dough with long, sharp knife into ¼-inch slices. Place 2 inches apart on *ungreased* cookie sheets.

6. Bake 10 minutes or until set. Let cookies stand on cookie sheets 2 minutes. Remove cookies with spatula to wire racks; cool.

7. Melt chocolate in 1-cup glass measure set in bowl of very hot water, stirring twice. This will take about 10 minutes. Dip each cookie into chocolate, coating 1 inch up sides. Let excess chocolate drip back into cup.

8. Transfer to wire racks or waxed paper; let stand at cool room temperature about 40 minutes until chocolate is set.

9. Store between sheets of waxed paper at cool room temperature or in refrigerator. Do not freeze.

Makes about 2 dozen cookies

Step 3. Forming a log.

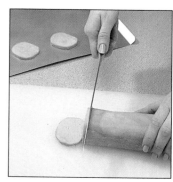
Step 5. Cutting dough into ¼-inch slices.

Step 7. Dipping cookies into melted chocolate.

White Chocolate Chunk Brownies

4 squares (1 ounce each)
   unsweetened chocolate,
   coarsely chopped
$\frac{1}{2}$ cup butter or margarine
2 large eggs
$1\frac{1}{4}$ cups granulated sugar
1 teaspoon vanilla
$\frac{1}{2}$ cup all-purpose flour
$\frac{1}{2}$ teaspoon salt
6 ounces white baking bar, cut
   into $\frac{1}{4}$-inch pieces
$\frac{1}{2}$ cup coarsely chopped walnuts
   (optional)
   Powdered sugar for garnish

1. Preheat oven to 350°F. Grease 8-inch square baking pan; set aside.

2. Melt unsweetened chocolate and butter in small, heavy saucepan over low heat, stirring constantly; set aside.

3. Beat eggs in large bowl with electric mixer at medium speed 30 seconds. Gradually add granulated sugar, beating at medium speed about 4 minutes until very thick and lemon colored.

4. Beat in chocolate mixture and vanilla. Beat in flour and salt at low speed just until blended. Stir in baking bar pieces and walnuts with mixing spoon. Spread batter evenly into prepared baking pan.

5. Bake 30 minutes or until edges just begin to pull away from sides of pan and center is set.

6. Remove pan to wire rack; cool completely. Cut into 2-inch squares. Place powdered sugar in fine-mesh strainer; sprinkle over brownies, if desired.

7. Store tightly covered at room temperature or freeze up to 3 months.

Makes 16 brownies

Step 3. Batter beaten to lemon color.

Step 4. Stirring in baking bar pieces.

Step 6. Sprinkling powdered sugar over brownies.

Fudgy Bittersweet Brownie Pie

12 ounces bittersweet chocolate candy bar, broken into pieces
½ cup butter or margarine
2 large eggs
½ cup sugar
1 cup all-purpose flour
½ teaspoon salt
  Vanilla ice cream
  Prepared hot fudge sauce
  Red and white candy sprinkles
    for garnish

1. Preheat oven to 350°F. Grease 10-inch tart pan with removable bottom or 9-inch square baking pan; set aside.

2. Melt chocolate and butter in small, heavy saucepan over low heat, stirring constantly; set aside.

3. Beat eggs in medium bowl with electric mixer at medium speed 30 seconds. Gradually beat in sugar; beat 1 minute.

4. Beat in chocolate mixture, scraping down side of bowl once. Beat in flour and salt at low speed until just combined, scraping down side of bowl once. Spread batter evenly in prepared baking pan.

5. Bake 25 minutes or until center is just set. Remove pan to wire rack; cool completely.

6. To serve, cut brownies into 12 wedges or 12 squares if using square pan. Top each piece with a scoop of vanilla ice cream. Place fudge sauce in small microwavable bowl or glass measuring cup. Microwave at HIGH until hot, stirring once. Spoon over ice cream; top with candy sprinkles, if desired.

7. Store leftover brownies tightly covered at room temperature or freeze up to 3 months.

Makes 16 brownies

Step 3. Adding sugar to beaten eggs.

Step 4. Scraping down side of bowl.

Step 6. Cutting into wedges.

Decadent Blonde Brownies

1 jar (3½ ounces) macadamia
  nuts
1½ cups all-purpose flour
 1 teaspoon baking powder
 ½ teaspoon salt
 ½ cup butter or margarine,
  softened
 ¾ cup granulated sugar
 ¾ cup packed light brown sugar
 2 large eggs
 2 teaspoons vanilla
 1 package (10 ounces) semisweet
  chocolate chunks*

*If chocolate chunks are not available, cut
10-ounce thick chocolate candy bar into
½-inch pieces to equal 1½ cups.

1. Preheat oven to 350°F. Well grease 13 × 9-inch baking pan; set aside.

2. Coarsely chop macadamia nuts with chef's knife to measure ¾ cup.

3. Place flour, baking powder and salt in small bowl; stir to combine.

4. Beat butter, granulated sugar and brown sugar in large bowl with electric mixer at medium speed until light and fluffy, scraping down side of bowl once. Beat in eggs and vanilla, scraping down side of bowl once. Add flour mixture. Beat at low speed until well blended, scraping down side of bowl once.

5. Stir in chocolate chunks and macadamia nuts with mixing spoon. Spread batter evenly into prepared baking pan.

6. Bake 25 to 30 minutes or until golden brown. Remove pan to wire rack; cool completely. Cut into 3¼ × 1½-inch bars.

7. Store tightly covered at room temperature or freeze up to 3 months.

Makes 2 dozen brownies

Step 2. Chopping macadamia nuts.

Step 5. Spreading batter in pan.

Step 6. Cutting into bars.

Coconut Crowned Cappuccino Brownies

6 squares (1 ounce each) semisweet chocolate, coarsely chopped
1 tablespoon freeze dried coffee
1 tablespoon boiling water
³/4 cup all-purpose flour
³/4 teaspoon ground cinnamon
¹/2 teaspoon baking powder
¹/4 teaspoon salt
¹/2 cup sugar
¹/4 cup butter or margarine, softened
3 large eggs, divided
¹/4 cup whipping cream
1 teaspoon vanilla
³/4 cup flaked coconut, divided
¹/2 cup semisweet chocolate chips, divided

1. Preheat oven to 350°F. Grease 8-inch square baking pan; set aside.

2. Melt chocolate squares in small, heavy saucepan over low heat, stirring constantly; set aside. Dissolve coffee in boiling water in small cup; set aside.

3. Place flour, cinnamon, baking powder and salt in small bowl; stir to combine.

4. Beat sugar and butter in large bowl with electric mixer at medium speed until light and fluffy, scraping down side of bowl. Beat in 2 eggs, 1 at a time, scraping down side of bowl after each addition. Beat in chocolate mixture and coffee mixture until well combined. Add flour mixture. Beat at low speed until well blended, scraping down side of bowl once. Spread batter evenly into prepared baking pan.

5. For topping, combine cream, remaining 1 egg and vanilla in small bowl; mix well. Stir in ¹/2 cup coconut and ¹/4 cup chips. Spread evenly over brownie base; sprinkle with remaining ¹/4 cup coconut and chips.

6. Bake 30 to 35 minutes or until coconut is browned and center is set. Remove pan to wire rack; cool completely. Cut into 2-inch squares.

7. Store tightly covered at room temperature or freeze up to 3 months.

Makes 16 brownies

Step 2. Stirring chocolate.

Step 5. Spreading topping over batter.

Butterscotch Brownies

1 cup butterscotch-flavored chips
1 cup all-purpose flour
1/2 teaspoon baking powder
1/4 teaspoon salt
1/4 cup butter or margarine, softened
1/2 cup packed light brown sugar
2 large eggs
1/2 teaspoon vanilla
1 cup semisweet chocolate chips
1 tablespoon unsweetened cocoa powder for garnish

1. Preheat oven to 350°F. Lightly grease 9-inch square baking pan; set aside.

2. Melt butterscotch-flavored chips in small, heavy saucepan over low heat, stirring constantly; set aside.

3. Place flour, baking powder and salt in small bowl; stir to combine.

4. Beat butter and sugar in large bowl with electric mixer at medium speed until light and fluffy, scraping down side of bowl once. Beat in eggs, 1 at a time, scraping down side of bowl after each addition. Beat in vanilla. Beat in melted butterscotch chips. Add flour mixture. Beat at low speed until well blended, scraping down side of bowl. Spread batter evenly into prepared baking pan.

5. Bake 20 to 25 minutes or until golden brown and center is set. Remove pan from oven and immediately sprinkle chocolate chips in single layer over brownies. Let stand about 4 minutes until chocolate is melted. Spread chocolate evenly over top of brownies with thin spatula. Slightly swirl chocolate, if desired.

6. Place pan on wire rack; cool completely.

7. To garnish, place small strips of cardboard over chocolate. Place cocoa in fine-mesh strainer; sprinkle over brownies. Carefully remove cardboard. Cut brownies into 2 1/4-inch squares.

8. Store tightly covered at room temperature or freeze up to 3 months.

Makes 16 brownies

Step 2. Melting and stirring butterscotch chips.

Step 4. Scraping down side of bowl.

Step 5. Spreading chocolate chips over hot brownies.

Minted Chocolate Chip Brownies

3/4 cup granulated sugar
1/2 cup butter or margarine
2 tablespoons water
1 cup semisweet chocolate chips
  or mini chocolate chips
1 1/2 teaspoons vanilla
1 1/4 cups all-purpose flour
1/2 teaspoon baking soda
1/2 teaspoon salt
2 large eggs
1 cup mint chocolate chips
  Powdered sugar for garnish

1. Preheat oven to 350°F. Grease 9-inch square baking pan; set aside.

2. Combine sugar, butter and water in medium microwavable mixing bowl. Microwave at HIGH 2 1/2 to 3 minutes or until butter is melted. Stir in semisweet chips; stir gently until chips are melted and mixture is well blended. Stir in vanilla; let stand 5 minutes to cool.

3. Place flour, baking soda and salt in small bowl; stir to combine.

4. Beat eggs into chocolate mixture, 1 at a time, with mixing spoon. Add flour mixture; mix well. Stir in mint chips. Spread batter evenly into prepared baking pan.

5. Bake 25 minutes for fudgy brownies or 30 to 35 minutes for cakelike brownies.

6. Remove pan to wire rack; cool completely. Cut into 2 1/4-inch squares. Place powdered sugar in fine-mesh strainer; sprinkle over brownies, if desired.

7. Store tightly covered at room temperature or freeze up to 3 months.

Makes 16 brownies

Step 2. Stirring chocolate chips in melted butter mixture.

Step 4. Beating in eggs, one at a time.

Step 6. Sprinkling powdered sugar over brownies.

Irish Brownies

1 cup all-purpose flour
$^{1}/_{2}$ teaspoon baking powder
$^{1}/_{4}$ teaspoon salt
4 squares (1 ounce each)
    semisweet baking chocolate,
    coarsely chopped
$^{1}/_{2}$ cup butter or margarine
$^{1}/_{2}$ cup sugar
2 large eggs
$^{1}/_{4}$ cup Irish cream liqueur
    Irish Cream Frosting (recipe
    follows)

1. Preheat oven to 350°F. Grease 8-inch square baking pan; set aside. Place flour, baking powder and salt in small bowl; stir.

2. Melt chocolate and butter in medium, heavy saucepan over low heat, stirring constantly. Stir in sugar. Beat in eggs, 1 at a time, with wire whisk. Whisk in liqueur. Whisk flour mixture into chocolate mixture until just blended. Spread batter evenly into prepared baking pan.

3. Bake 22 to 25 minutes or until center is set. Remove pan to wire rack; cool completely before frosting.

4. Prepare Irish Cream Frosting. Spread frosting over cooled brownies. Chill at least 1 hour or until frosting is set. Cut into 2-inch squares.

5. Store tightly covered in refrigerator. These brownies do not freeze well.

Makes 16 brownies

Step 2. Whisking in eggs, one at a time.

Irish Cream Frosting

Powdered sugar
2 ounces cream cheese ($^{1}/_{4}$ cup), softened
2 tablespoons butter or margarine, softened
2 tablespoons Irish cream liqueur

1. Sift powdered sugar with sifter or fine-mesh strainer onto waxed paper. Gently spoon into measuring cups to measure $1^{1}/_{2}$ cups.

2. Beat cream cheese and butter in small bowl with electric mixer at medium speed until smooth, scraping down side of bowl once. Beat in liqueur. Gradually beat in powdered sugar until smooth.

Makes about $^{2}/_{3}$ cup

Irish Cream Frosting:
Step 1. Sifting powdered sugar.

Checkerboard Bars

½ cup hazelnuts (2½ ounces)
4 ounces bittersweet or
   semisweet chocolate candy
   bar, broken into pieces
2¼ cups all-purpose flour
½ teaspoon baking powder
¼ teaspoon salt
¾ cup butter or margarine,
   softened
¾ cup sugar
2 large eggs, divided
1 teaspoon vanilla

1. Preheat oven to 350°F. To remove skins from hazelnuts, spread hazelnuts in single layer on baking sheet. Bake 10 to 12 minutes until toasted and skins begin to flake off; let cool slightly. Wrap hazelnuts in heavy kitchen towel; rub against towel to remove as much of the skins as possible.

2. Place hazelnuts in food processor. Process using on/off pulsing action until hazelnuts are finely chopped, but not pasty.

3. Melt chocolate in small bowl set in bowl of very hot water, stirring twice. This will take about 10 minutes.

4. Place flour, baking powder and salt in medium bowl; stir to combine.

5. Beat butter and sugar in large bowl with electric mixer at medium speed until light and fluffy, scraping down side of bowl once. Beat in 1 egg and vanilla, scraping down side of bowl once. Gradually add flour mixture. Beat at low speed, scraping down side of bowl occasionally.

6. Remove and reserve 1¼ cups dough. Stir chocolate and nuts into remaining dough with mixing spoon. Wrap both doughs in plastic wrap and refrigerate 20 minutes.

7. Unwrap chocolate dough. Place on lightly floured surface. Roll out to ⅓-inch thickness with floured rolling pin. Cut dough into eight 4 × ¾-inch strips. Reroll scraps as necessary, until all dough has been cut into strips. Repeat process with vanilla dough.

continued on page 76

Step 1. Rubbing hazelnuts to remove skins.

Step 6. Making chocolate dough.

Step 7. Cutting dough into strips.

Checkerboard Bars, continued

8. To assemble, beat remaining egg in small dish with fork until frothy. Place one strip of chocolate dough on sheet of plastic wrap. Brush edge with egg. Place one strip of vanilla dough next to chocolate dough. Brush edge with egg. Repeat with one more chocolate strip and one more vanilla strip to make bottom layer. Brush top with egg.

9. Prepare second row by stacking strips on first row, alternating vanilla dough over chocolate and chocolate over vanilla dough. Brush edge of each strip and top layer with egg. Repeat with third row to complete 1 checkerboard bar. Repeat entire process with remaining dough strips to complete second checkerboard bar. Cover with plastic wrap; refrigerate 1 hour or until firm enough to slice.

10. Preheat oven to 350°F. Grease cookie sheets.

11. Unwrap checkerboard bar and cut crosswise with long, sharp knife into ¹/₄-inch slices. Place 2 inches apart on prepared cookie sheets.

12. Bake 10 to 12 minutes or until set. Cool cookies on cookie sheets 2 minutes. Remove cookies with spatula to wire racks; cool completely.

13. Store tightly covered at room temperature or freeze up to 3 months.

Makes 2 dozen bars

Step 8. Arranging first row of checkerboard.

Step 9. Brushing edge of strip with beaten egg.

Step 11. Cutting checkerboard into ¹/₄-inch slices.

Viennese Meringue Bars

½ cup slivered almonds
3 large eggs
1 cup butter or margarine,
    softened
1¼ cups sugar, divided
¼ teaspoon salt
2¼ cups all-purpose flour
1 cup seedless raspberry jam
1½ cups mini semisweet chocolate
    chips

1. Preheat oven to 350°F. To toast almonds, spread on baking sheet. Bake 8 to 10 minutes or until golden brown, stirring frequently. Remove almonds from pan and cool.

2. To separate egg yolks from whites, gently tap egg in center against hard surface, such as side of bowl. Holding a shell half in each hand, gently transfer yolk back and forth between the 2 halves. Allow white to drip down between the 2 halves into bowl. When all white has dripped into bowl, place yolk in another bowl. (Whites must be free of any egg yolk to reach the proper volume when beaten.) Transfer white to third bowl. Repeat with remaining eggs.

3. Store 1 egg yolk, covered with water, in airtight container for another use. Refrigerate up to 3 days.

4. Preheat oven to 350°F.

5. Beat butter and ½ cup sugar in large bowl with electric mixer at medium speed until light and fluffy, scraping down side of bowl once. Beat in 2 egg yolks and salt. Gradually add flour. Beat at low speed, scraping down side of bowl once.

6. With buttered fingers, pat dough evenly into *ungreased* 15 × 10-inch jelly-roll pan.

continued on page 78

Step 1. Toasting almonds.

Step 2. Separating an egg.

Step 6. Patting dough into pan.

Viennese Meringue Bars, continued

7. Bake 22 to 25 minutes or until light golden brown. Remove from oven; immediately spread jam over crust. Sprinkle evenly with chocolate chips.

8. To make the meringue topping, beat egg whites in clean large bowl with electric mixer on high speed until foamy. Gradually beat in remaining ¾ cup sugar until stiff peaks form. (After beaters are lifted from egg white mixture, stiff peaks should remain on surface, and when bowl is tilted, mixture will not slide around.)

9. Fold in almonds with rubber spatula by gently cutting down to the bottom of the bowl, scraping up the side of the bowl, then folding over the top of the mixture. Repeat until almonds are evenly incorporated into the meringue.

10. Spoon meringue over chocolate mixture; spread evenly with small spatula.

11. Return pan to oven; bake 20 to 25 minutes until golden brown. Transfer pan to wire rack; cool completely. Cut into 2 × 2½-inch bars.

12. Store loosely covered at room temperature. These cookies do not freeze well.

Makes 28 bars

Step 8. Egg whites beaten to stiff peaks.

Step 9. Folding in almonds.

Step 10. Spreading meringue over base.

Cinnamon Nut Chocolate Spirals

1½ cups all-purpose flour
¼ teaspoon salt
⅓ cup butter or margarine, softened
¾ cup sugar, divided
1 large egg
1 cup mini semisweet chocolate chips
1 cup very finely chopped walnuts
2 teaspoons ground cinnamon
3 tablespoons butter or margarine, melted

1. Place flour and salt in small bowl; stir to combine. Beat softened butter and ½ cup sugar in large bowl with electric mixer at medium speed until light and fluffy, scraping down side of bowl once. Beat in egg. Gradually add flour mixture, mixing with mixing spoon. Dough will be stiff. (If necessary, knead dough by hand until it holds together.)

2. Roll out dough between 2 sheets of waxed paper into 12 × 10-inch rectangle. Remove waxed paper from top of rectangle. (Techniques on pages 53 and 54.)

3. Combine chips, walnuts, remaining ¼ cup sugar and cinnamon in medium bowl. Pour hot melted butter over mixture; mix well. (Chocolate will partially melt.) Spoon mixture over dough. Spread evenly with small spatula, leaving ½-inch border on long edges.

4. Using bottom sheet of waxed paper as a guide and starting at long side, tightly roll up dough jelly-roll style, removing waxed paper as you roll. Wrap in plastic wrap; refrigerate 30 minutes to 1 hour.*

5. Preheat oven to 350°F. Lightly grease cookie sheets. Unwrap dough. Using heavy thread or dental floss, cut dough into ½-inch slices. Place slices 2 inches apart on prepared cookie sheets.

6. Bake 14 minutes or until edges are light golden brown. Remove cookies with spatula to wire racks; cool.

7. Store tightly covered at room temperature or freeze up to 3 months.

Makes about 2 dozen cookies

*If dough is chilled longer than 1 hour, slice with a sharp, thin knife.

Step 4. Rolling up dough jelly-roll style.

Step 5. Cutting dough into ½-inch slices with dental floss.

Peek-A-Boo
Apricot Cookies

4 ounces bittersweet chocolate
  candy bar, broken into pieces
3 cups all-purpose flour
1/2 teaspoon baking soda
1/2 teaspoon salt
2/3 cup butter or margarine,
  softened
3/4 cup sugar
2 large eggs
2 teaspoons vanilla
  Apricot preserves

1. Melt chocolate in small bowl set in bowl of very hot water, stirring twice. This will take about 10 minutes.

2. Place flour, baking soda and salt in medium bowl; stir to combine.

3. Beat butter and sugar in large bowl with electric mixer at medium speed until light and fluffy, scraping down side of bowl once. Beat in eggs, 1 at a time, scraping down side of bowl after each addition. Beat in vanilla and chocolate. Slowly add flour mixture. Beat at low speed, scraping down side of bowl once.

4. Divide dough into 2 rounds; flatten into discs. Wrap in plastic wrap; refrigerate 2 hours or until firm.

5. Preheat oven to 350°F. Unwrap dough; roll out to 1/4- to 1/8-inch thickness on lightly floured surface with floured rolling pin. Cut out dough with 2 1/2-inch-round cutter. Cut 1-inch centers out of half the circles. Remove scraps of dough from around and within circles; reserve. Place circles on *ungreased* cookie sheets. Repeat rolling and cutting with remaining scraps of dough.

6. Bake cookies 9 to 10 minutes or until set. Let cookies stand on cookie sheets 2 minutes. Remove cookies with spatula to wire rack; cool completely.

7. To assemble cookies, spread about 1 1/2 teaspoons preserves over flat side of cookie circles; top with cut-out cookies to form a sandwich.

8. Store tightly covered at room temperature. These cookies do not freeze well.

Makes about 1 1/2 dozen cookies

Step 1. Melting chocolate in a bowl set in very hot water.

Step 5. Cutting out centers from cookies.

Step 7. Assembling cookies.

Chocolate Chip Almond Biscotti

1 cup sliced almonds
2¾ cups all-purpose flour
1½ teaspoons baking powder
¼ teaspoon salt
½ cup butter or margarine, softened
1 cup sugar
3 large eggs
3 tablespoons almond-flavored liqueur
1 tablespoon water
1 cup mini semisweet chocolate chips

1. Preheat oven to 350°F. To toast almonds, spread on baking sheet. Bake 8 to 10 minutes or until golden brown, stirring frequently. Remove almonds; cool. Coarsely chop nuts with chef's knife to measure ¾ cup.

2. Place flour, baking powder and salt in medium bowl; stir to combine.

3. Beat butter and sugar in large bowl with electric mixer at medium speed until light and fluffy, scraping down side of bowl once. Beat in eggs, 1 at a time, scraping down side of bowl after each addition. Beat in liqueur and water. Gradually add flour mixture. Beat at low speed, scraping down side of bowl occasionally. Stir in chips and almonds.

4. Divide dough into fourths. Spread each quarter evenly down center of a sheet of waxed paper. Using waxed paper to hold dough, roll it back and forth to form a 15-inch log. (Technique on page 58.) Wrap securely. Refrigerate about 2 hours or until firm.

5. Preheat oven to 375°F. Lightly grease cookie sheet. Unwrap and place each log on prepared cookie sheet. With floured hands, shape each log 2 inches wide and ½ inch thick.

6. Bake 15 minutes. Remove from oven. Cut each log with serrated knife into 1-inch diagonal slices. Place slices, cut side up, on cookie sheet; bake 7 minutes. Turn cookies over; bake 7 minutes or until cut surfaces are golden brown and cookies are dry. Remove cookies with spatula to wire racks; cool.

7. Store tightly covered at room temperature or freeze up to 3 months.

Makes about 4 dozen cookies

Step 5. Shaping log on cookie sheet.

Step 6. Cutting into diagonal slices.

Cardamom-Chocolate Sandwiches

1½ cups all-purpose flour
1 teaspoon ground cardamom
½ teaspoon baking soda
½ teaspoon salt
¾ cup butter or margarine, softened
¾ cup firmly packed light brown sugar
¼ cup half-and-half
½ cup milk chocolate chips
2 tablespoons butter
2 tablespoons milk
1 cup sifted powdered sugar

1. Place flour, cardamom, baking soda and salt in small bowl; stir to combine.

2. Beat ¾ cup butter and brown sugar with electric mixer at medium speed until light and fluffy, scraping down side of bowl once. Beat in half-and-half, scraping down side of bowl once. Gradually add flour mixture. Beat at low speed, scraping down side of bowl once.

3. Spoon dough down center of sheet of waxed paper. Using waxed paper to hold dough, roll it back and forth to form a tight, smooth 10-inch round log. (Technique on page 58.) If dough is too soft to form a tight log, refrigerate 1 hour and reroll log until smooth. Wrap securely. Refrigerate about 4 hours or until firm. (Dough may be kept refrigerated up to 3 days.)

4. Preheat oven to 375°F. Unwrap dough; cut into ¼-inch slices with long, sharp knife. Place 2 inches apart on *ungreased* cookie sheets.

5. Bake 10 to 12 minutes or until edges are golden brown and cookies are set. Let cookies stand on cookie sheets 2 minutes. Remove cookies with spatula to wire racks; cool completely.

6. For icing, place chips and 2 tablespoons butter in small microwavable bowl. Microwave at HIGH 1½ minutes or until melted, stirring after 1 minute. Stir in milk until smooth. Beat in powdered sugar.

7. Spread filling over bottom side of half the cookies; top with remaining cookies.

8. Store tightly covered at room temperature or freeze up to 3 months.

Makes about 1 dozen cookies

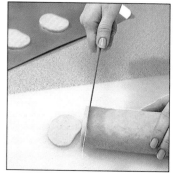

Step 4. Cutting dough into ¼-inch slices.

Step 7. Spreading filling on cookies.

Chocolate-Raspberry Kolachy

2 squares (1 ounce each) semisweet chocolate, coarsely chopped
1½ cups all-purpose flour
¼ teaspoon baking soda
¼ teaspoon salt
½ cup butter or margarine, softened
3 ounces cream cheese or light cream cheese, softened
⅓ cup granulated sugar
1 teaspoon vanilla
Seedless raspberry jam
Powdered sugar

1. Preheat oven to 375°F. Lightly grease cookie sheets. Place chocolate in 1-cup glass measure. Microwave at HIGH 3 to 4 minutes or until chocolate is melted, stirring after 2 minutes; set aside.

2. Place flour, baking soda and salt in small bowl; stir. Beat butter and cream cheese in large bowl with electric mixer at medium speed until well blended, scraping down side of bowl occasionally. Beat in granulated sugar until light and fluffy, scraping down side of bowl once. Beat in vanilla and chocolate. Gradually add flour mixture. Beat at low speed, scraping down side of bowl once.

3. Divide dough in half; flatten each piece into a disc. Wrap in plastic wrap. Refrigerate about 2 hours or until firm.

4. Unwrap and roll out each piece of dough to ¼- to ⅛-inch thickness on well-floured surface with floured rolling pin. Cut out with 3-inch round biscuit cutter. Place 2 inches apart on cookie sheets. Place rounded ½ teaspoon jam in center of each circle.

5. Bring three edges of dough up over jam; pinch edges together to seal, leaving center of triangle slightly open.

6. Bake 10 minutes or until set. Let cookies stand on cookie sheets 2 minutes. Remove cookies with spatula to wire racks; cool completely. Just before serving, sprinkle with powdered sugar.

7. Store tightly covered in refrigerator; let stand 30 minutes at room temperature before serving. These cookies do not freeze well.

Makes about 18 cookies

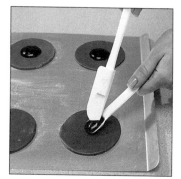

Step 4. Placing jam on dough.

Step 5. Shaping dough into triangle.

Chocolate Edged Lace Cookies

2 large eggs
2/3 cup ground almonds
1/2 cup butter
1/2 cup sugar
1/3 cup all-purpose flour
2 tablespoons heavy cream
1/4 teaspoon salt
4 ounces dark sweet or bittersweet chocolate candy bar, broken into pieces

1. Preheat oven to 375°F. Well grease cookie sheet; set aside.

2. Spread ground almonds onto baking sheet. Bake 5 minutes or until light golden brown and fragrant.

3. Combine butter, sugar, flour, cream and salt in medium, heavy saucepan. Add almonds; cook over medium heat, stirring constantly, about 5 minutes or until butter melts and small bubbles form around sides of saucepan. Remove from heat; stir well.

4. Drop rounded teaspoonfuls of batter 6 inches apart on prepared cookie sheet. (Bake only 4 cookies per sheet.)

5. Bake 6 to 8 minutes or until cookies are deep golden brown around edges. Let cookies stand on cookie sheet 2 minutes. Remove cookies with spatula to wire rack;* cool.

6. Melt chocolate in small, heavy saucepan over low heat, stirring constantly. Tilt saucepan to pool chocolate at one end; dip edge of each cookie in chocolate, turning cookie slowly so entire edge is tinged with chocolate.

7. Let cookies stand on waxed paper until chocolate is set.

8. Store tightly covered at room temperature. Do not freeze.

Makes about 2½ dozen cookies

*For tuile-shaped cookies, balance a wooden spoon over two cans of the same height. Working quickly while cookies are still hot, drape the cookies over the handle of the spoon so that both sides hang down and form a taco shape; cool completely. Dip both edges of cookies into chocolate.

Step 4. Placing teaspoonfuls of batter on cookie sheet.

Step 6. Dipping edge of cookie in melted chocolate.

Tuile-shaped cookies: Shaping cookies.

Choco-Cherry Cookies Supreme

$2/3$ cup all-purpose flour
$1/2$ cup unsweetened cocoa powder
$1^1/2$ teaspoons baking powder
$1/2$ teaspoon salt
$1/3$ cup butter or margarine, softened
$1/2$ cup granulated sugar
$1/2$ cup packed light brown sugar
$1/3$ cup milk
1 large egg
1 teaspoon vanilla
2 cups uncooked quick-cooking or old-fashioned oats
3 ounces white baking bar or white chocolate candy bar, cut into $1/4$-inch pieces
$1/2$ cup candied cherries, cut into halves

1. Preheat oven to 375°F. Lightly grease cookie sheets; set aside.

2. Place flour, cocoa, baking powder and salt in small bowl; stir to combine.

3. Beat butter, granulated sugar and brown sugar in large bowl with electric mixer at medium speed until light and fluffy, scraping down side of bowl once. Beat in milk, egg and vanilla, scraping down side of bowl once. Gradually add flour mixture. Beat at low speed, scraping down side of bowl occasionally.

4. Stir in oats with mixing spoon until well blended. Stir in baking bar pieces and cherries.

5. Drop heaping teaspoonfuls of dough 2 inches apart onto prepared cookie sheets.

6. Bake 10 minutes or until set. Let cookies stand on cookie sheets 1 minute. Remove cookies with spatula to wire racks; cool completely.

7. Store tightly covered at room temperature or freeze up to 3 months.

Makes about 3 dozen cookies

Step 4. Stirring in baking bar pieces and cherries.

Step 5. Placing heaping teaspoonfuls of dough on cookie sheets.

Step 6. Removing cookies to wire rack.

INDEX